LOOK WHAT I MADE

Interactive Nature Activities for Young Children

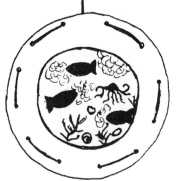

Over 40 Craft Ideas

Over 120 Related Activities

Joan Wheaton Buma

Prima Publishing
P.O. Box 1260JWB2
Rocklin, CA 95677
(916) 786-0449

To My Grandmother Laura Mogg...

....who dragged her mattress out to the porch so "us kids" could sleep under the stars, who always provided an enthusiastic audience for our backyard performances, who turned every summer holiday into sheer delight. Thanks, Nana.

MANY THANKS TO...

- John, my husband, for his unwavering support and love
- My children—Mark, Sarah, and Jonathan—for being such eager participants in all the activities presented in this book
- My mother, whose poetic talent was invaluable in the creating of this book
- My father, whose generosity made this venture possible
- My sister, Mary, who provided the title
- Mary Ann Yacobucci, my brainstorming partner, whose ideas can be found throughout this book
- Tine Buma, for the gift of her poem, "The Warbler"
- Family and friends, for their encouragement and suggestions

©1992 by Joan Wheaton Buma

Prima Publishing
Rocklin, CA

Library of Congress Cataloging-in-Publication Data
Buma, Joan Wheaton
    Look what I made now! : interactive nature activities for young children / by Joan Buma.
        p.   cm.
    Includes index.
    ISBN 1-55958-176-X
    1. Natural history—Study and teaching.   2. Nature study.
I. Title.
QH51.B86   1992   91-39331
372.3′57—dc20   CIP

92 93 94 95 RRD 10 9 8 7 6 5 4 3 2 1

Printed in the United States of America

PREFACE

As far back as I can remember, the enjoyment of nature has been an important aspect of my life. From hiking with my father during my childhood in the Ottawa Valley to present-day meanderings with my own children, I have marveled at nature. Out of this love for nature and my ongoing interest in children's activities evolved my second book, *Look What I Made Now!*

During the time I wrote this book, our three children ranged in age from 3 to 9. To accommodate this broad range, I developed open-ended activities simplistic enough for a 3-year-old, but that also allowed room for the creative flair of a 9-year-old. Unlike *Look What I Made!*, which was geared to preschoolers, the activities in this book will appeal to children of all ages.

Once again I have used a thematic approach. Having taught for a number of years in the elementary grades, I remain convinced that learning is much more fun, natural, and meaningful when conceptually integrated. Each craft and the accompanying related activities have a common theme. The craft is not only a child's creation, but it becomes part of his or her play through verses, songs, games, and other learning experiences.

The activities presented in this book are not meant to be an end in themselves, but rather a vehicle for nurturing children and helping them to develop self-confidence. All the activities require materials that are simple and readily available—in fact, many can be found in your own backyard. Each activity has been child-tested and thoroughly enjoyed.

This book responds to a child's natural love and curiosity for animals and the surrounding environment. It also touches upon the fragile nature of our environment and how we need to care for it.

The next time you're wondering what to so with one child or a group of children, just look around you at the wealth of materials in the environment—nature at hand.

Joan Wheaton Bumma

CONTENTS

NATURE'S CREATURES

THUMBPRINT LADYBUGS

MATERIALS:
- White paper
- Red paint
- Green construction paper
- Glue
- Thin black markers (or crayons)
- Scissors
- Shallow container or containers

PREPARATION:
- *Cut grass strips out of green construction paper.*
- *Place red paint in a shallow container or containers.*

CHILD'S PLAY:
- *Place your thumb in the red paint and then place it on the white paper. Make anywhere from 5 to 10 well-spaced red thumbprints per sheet.*
- *Allow time for paint to dry. (This is a good opportunity to try the related activities.)*
- *Use a black marker or crayon on the thumbprints to make the features of a ladybug. (See illustration below.)*
- *Glue grass strips among the ladybugs on the paper.*

  VARIATION: Instead of green construction paper, use green paint and little fingers to create blades of grass.

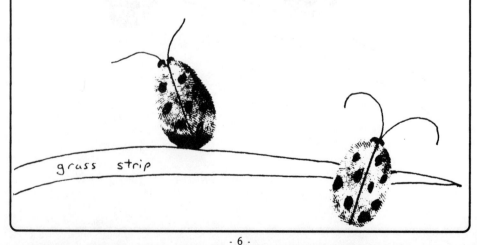

grass strip

Related Activities

1. NURSERY RHYME:

Decorate each child's red thumb with the black marker to create ladybugs. The children can use their thumbs to act out the following verse:

LADYBUG, LADYBUG, FLY AWAY HOME,
YOUR HOUSE IS ON FIRE,
YOUR CHILDREN WILL BURN.

2. ACTION SONG:

Sing to the tune of "Five Green and Speckled Frogs."

FIVE SPECKLED LADYBUGS,
SAT ON A SPECKLED RUG,
EATING SOME MOST DELICIOUS GRASS,
YUM! YUM!
ONE FLEW UP IN THE SKY
WHERE IT WAS NICE AND HIGH,
THEN THERE WERE FOUR SPECKLED LADYBUGS.

FOUR SPECKLED LADYBUGS...

3. SNACK TIME: *Apple Ladybugs*

Give each child half an apple, two toothpicks, and two miniature marshmallows. Antennae can be made by sticking the toothpicks into the apple, and the marshmallows into the tops of the toothpicks. The children will enjoy making their own delicious, nutritious, ladybug snacks.

4. OUTDOOR FUN:

In warm weather go on a ladybug hunt. Where do you think they like to hide? If you have a magnifying glass, this would be a good time to put it to use.

20,000 LEAGUES UNDER THE SEA

MATERIALS:

- Paper plates
- Construction paper
- Shoelaces (or yarn)
- Crayons
- Clear plastic wrap
- Glue
- Small seashells (optional)
- One-hole punch
- Scissors
- Masking tape (optional)

PREPARATION:

- *Punch holes around the perimeter of two paper plates. (Punch the holes with the plates together so the holes line up. Holes should be approx. 1½" (4 cm) apart.) Provide two plates per child.*
- *Cut a large circle out of the center of one of the paper plates. This becomes paper plate B; the other is plate A.*
- *Trace and cut fish from construction paper (three fish per child.)*

CHILD'S PLAY:

- *Color the inside surface of paper plate A with blue crayon.*
- *Glue on precut fish and small shells, if available.*
- *Complete the underwater scene by using crayons; draw seaweed, shells, octopus, etc.*
- *Glue a piece of clear plastic wrap on the inside of paper plate B, covering the hole.*
- *Lace the two paper plates together by going in and out of the holes with a shoelace or yarn (wrap the end in masking tape for easy threading).*

  VARIATION: Instead of coloring the background with a crayon, make blue bubble prints (see p. 66) on paper plate A.

Related Activities

1. FINGERPLAY:

THREE LITTLE FISHES SIDE BY SIDE, (show three fingers)
SWIM THROUGH THE WATER,
SWIM THROUGH THE TIDE. (swimming motion)
THEY DON'T NEED A MOTOR (shake head)
AND THEY DON'T PUT UP A SAIL,
THEY JUST WIGGLE THEIR FINS (wiggle hands together)
AND FLIP THEIR TAILS.

2. SONG:

Sing to the tune of "Mary Had a Little Lamb."

LOOK THROUGH THE SUBMARINE WINDOW,
WINDOW, WINDOW.
LOOK THROUGH THE SUBMARINE WINDOW,
WHAT DO YOU SEE?

Each child can hold his or her craft and take a turn telling about something in the window or that the child might see through a submarine window.

3. NURSERY RHYME:

ONE, TWO, THREE, FOUR, FIVE,
I CAUGHT A LITTLE FISH ALIVE.
WHY DID YOU LET IT GO?
BECAUSE IT BIT MY FINGER SO.
WHICH FINGER DID IT BITE?
THE LITTLE FINGER ON THE RIGHT.

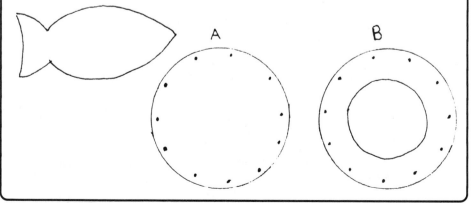

FANCIFUL BUTTERFLY

MATERIALS:

- Fingerpaint paper
  (or white glossy paper)
- Fingerpaint (see recipe p. 11)
- Black construction paper
- Glue
- Scissors

PREPARATION:

- *You can purchase fingerpaint or make your own. We used the primary colors: red, yellow, and just a touch of blue.*
- *Cut a butterfly frame out of black construction paper.*
- *Moisten fingerpaint paper when ready to start.*

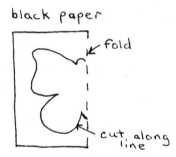

black paper

fold

cut along line

CHILD'S PLAY:

- *Put a dab of (red) paint on your fingerpaint paper and use your fingers to spread the paint.*
- *Try using your knuckles, fingernails, and the sides of your hands to create beautiful swirls.*
- *Add (yellow) paint, using the same technique.*
- *Finally, with a small dab of (blue) paint on the end of your finger, add a few highlights.*
- *Glue the black construction paper frame to your picture, and—voilà—a beautiful butterfly.*

HINT: Young children need help aligning their frames. Finished butterflies look beautiful hanging on a window.

Related Activities

1. ACTION VERSE:

IF I WERE A BUTTERFLY,
MY PRETTY WINGS I'D SPREAD.
I'D VISIT EVERY FLOWER,
AND NEVER GO TO BED.

2. FINGERPAINT RECIPE:

1 cup (250 ml) flour
1 tsp. salt
3 cups (750 ml) cold water
3 jars (approx. 2-cup (500-ml) capacity) with lids
Powdered tempera

- *Mix flour, salt, and water together in the top of a double boiler.*
- *Cook until thick.*
- *Remove from heat and beat for 1 min. with electric mixer.*
- *Spoon goo into jars, and stir a tsp. of tempera into each.*

Note: *We used red, yellow, and blue since they produce the other colors when mixed together—much to a child's delight!*

- *Attach lids tightly and store in refrigerator.*

3. MONARCH BUTTERFLY:

Use the black butterfly shapes, left over from the black construction paper frames, and orange tissue paper to create monarch butterflies. Children can tear small pieces of the tissue paper and glue it onto the black butterfly shapes. Soon you will have a mural of monarchs.

LITTLE DUCK

MATERIALS:

- Clothespins
- White glue
- Feathers
- Black markers or crayons
- Yellow and orange construction paper
- Scissors

PREPARATION:

- *Trace ducks' bodies on the yellow construction paper and cut out the shapes.*
- *Trace beaks and legs on the orange construction paper and cut out the shapes.*

CHILD'S PLAY:

- *Glue the top of the beak to the outside upper edge of the pincer end of the clothespin (see Diagram A).*
- *Glue the bottom of the beak to the outside lower edge of the clothespin.*
- *Use a black marker or crayon to draw the duck's eye on the duck's head.*
- *Glue feet to duck's body, one foot behind the body and the other in front.*
- *Glue the feather to the tail end of the duck.*
- *Glue the duck's head to the clothespin (see Diagram B).*
- *Allow glue to dry, then make your duck quack by pinching the clothespin.*

VARIATION: Paint the clothespin orange rather than gluing on the beak. This method requires less fine motor control and is easier for the very young. You can also use brass fasteners to attach the legs to the duck's body, allowing increased mobility.

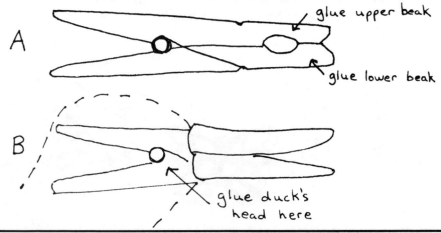

A — glue upper beak / glue lower beak

B — glue duck's head here

Related Activities

1. SONG:

SIX LITTLE DUCKS THAT I ONCE KNEW—
FAT ONES, SKINNY ONES, FAIR ONES TOO.
BUT THE ONE LITTLE DUCK WITH THE FEATHER ON
*   HIS BACK,*
HE LED THE OTHERS WITH HIS QUACK, QUACK, QUACK
QUACK, QUACK, QUACK;
HE LED THE OTHERS WITH HIS QUACK, QUACK, QUACK.
DOWN TO THE RIVER THEY WOULD GO—
WIBBLE, WOBBLE, WIBBLE, WOBBLE, TO AND FRO.
BUT THE ONE LITTLE DUCK WITH THE FEATHER ON
*   HIS BACK,*
HE LED THE OTHERS WITH HIS QUACK, QUACK, QUACK
QUACK, QUACK, QUACK;
HE LED THE OTHERS WITH HIS QUACK, QUACK, QUACK.

Have the children make their little ducks by
squeezing the clothespins.

2. BOOK: *Three Little Ducks Went Wandering*
by Ron Roy

This book is sure to captivate preschoolers.

← orange ↑

yellow

TWO LITTLE BLACKBIRDS

MATERIALS:
- Egg carton
- Yellow pipe cleaners
- Black paint
- Paintbrushes
- Commercial eyes, or self-stick circles (optional)
- Scissors, pencils

PREPARATION:
- *Cut two single "eggcups" (per child) from the egg carton.*
- *Cut the pipe cleaner into lengths of approx. 3" (7 cm).*
- *Use the pointed end of scissors to poke two holes into each eggcup (see Diagram A).*

CHILD'S PLAY:
- *Paint the two eggcups black, and allow them to dry. (Try some related activities.)*
- *Push one end of the pipe cleaner through one small hole and the other end of the pipe cleaner through the other hole.*
- *Pinch pipe cleaner to make a pointed beak.*
- *Repeat for the second blackbird.*
- *Now use commercial eyes or self-stick circles, felt, chalk— whatever you have handy—to make eyes for your blackbird.*
- *Poke a hole in the top of each cut by pushing a pencil through it. (The hole should be about the size of your "pointer" finger.)*
- *Try on your Two Little Blackbird finger puppets for size.*

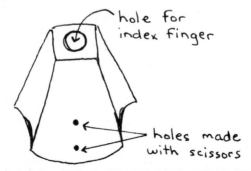

hole for index finger

holes made with scissors

Related Activities

1. ACTION VERSE:

Place the two blackbirds that you made on your pointer fingers and act out this verse:

TWO LITTLE BLACKBIRDS SITTING ON A HILL,

(hold each pointer finger in front of you)

ONE NAMED JACK, THE OTHER NAMED JILL.

(wiggle each bird in turn)

FLY AWAY, JACK; FLY AWAY, JILL.

(alternately put fingers behind your back)

COME BACK, JACK; COME BACK, JILL.

(return fingers, one at a time, in front of you)

VARIATION: The children can act out this verse by pretending they are blackbirds.

2. NURSERY RHYME:

*SING A SONG OF SIXPENCE
A POCKET FULL OF RYE;
FOUR-AND-TWENTY BLACKBIRDS
BAKED IN A PIE.*

*WHEN THE PIE WAS OPENED
THE BIRDS BEGAN TO SING;
WAS NOT THAT A DAINTY DISH
TO SET BEFORE THE KING?*

3. OUTDOOR FUN:

Feed the blackbirds and other birds by scattering birdseed or bread crumbs outdoors. Children never tire of feeding the birds.

FROG PUPPET

MATERIALS:
- Small flat-bottomed paper bag
- Green, yellow, and red construction paper
- Glue
- Black markers or crayons
- Scissors

PREPARATION:
- *Trace on the construction paper the shapes below; cut out the shapes. Provide one set of shapes per child.*

CHILD'S PLAY:
- *Glue tongue under the fold in the bag.*
- *Glue green eyes at the top of the fold.*
- *Glue yellow centers on top of the green eyes.*
- *Glue on front legs where the fold meets the bag.*
- *Glue haunches to the back of the bag.*
- *Add details—such as pupils, nostrils, and speckles—with the black marker or crayon.*

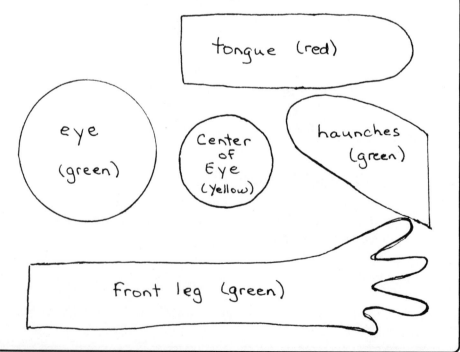

tongue (red)

eye (green)

Center of Eye (yellow)

haunches (green)

Front leg (green)

Related Activities

1. STORY TIME: *"Tad and Tessie"*

(This is a story of two little frogs as told by my grandmother to her children and grandchildren. It is now a favorite of her great grandchildren. Use the frog to help tell this delightful story.)

Tad and Tessie were two little frogs. They lived under Farmer Brown's back porch. One morning they were on their way to the barn to catch flies when suddenly they spotted a hawk soaring overhead. They hopped back to the safety of the back porch as fast as their little legs would take them. They knew that hawks like to eat little frogs!

Poor Tad and Tessie. Now they were so disappointed. They loved to catch flies at the barn. Then Tad had an idea. "I know," he said excitedly, "when Farmer Brown goes to milk the cow, we can hop into his milking pail." Tessie agreed that this was a fine idea.

Before too long, they heard Farmer Brown come whistling down the path.

"Get ready, Tessie," warned Tad.

"I'm ready!" HOP. Tessie landed in the pail, HOP—but where was Tad? Tessie couldn't find him anywhere!

At the barn, Farmer Brown set down the milking pail and hung his jacket on the hook. Tessie hopped out and looked high and low for Tad.

Meanwhile, Farmer Brown sat down on the stool and began to milk Bessie, the cow. P-shh, p-shh, p-shh, p-shh! He suddenly stopped. "Why, I thought I saw my jacket move," he said in amazement.

Bessie the cow replied, "Moo, moo—it's true, it's true." The little chick said, "Chick, chick—you better look quick."

Farmer Brown went to take a look, and who should he find in his jacket but Tad. "How did you get there, little frog?" he asked. He set Tad down on the barn floor, where he soon found Tessie. Tad was so happy to see Tessie. And Tessie was so happy to see Tad. They had a great time the rest of the day, catching flies in the barn.

GRAY SQUIRREL

MATERIALS:

- White bristol board
- Gray yarn
- White glue
- Paintbrushes
- Brass paper fasteners
- Crayons
- Scissors (or razor knife)

PREPARATION:

- *Trace and cut out the necessary shapes from bristol board.*
- *Poke a hole in the squirrel's body and tail to fasten them together later. Cut a slit in the body where the nut will fit.*
- *Cut yarn into small pieces of approx. 1" (2 cm) each. Cut lots—the bushier the tail the better!*

CHILD'S PLAY:

- *Brush white glue over the surface of the tail.*
- *Cover the glue with the pieces of yarn.*
- *Color squirrel's body with a crayon.*
- *Use crayons to add finishing touches—eyes, whiskers, etc.*
- *Color nut and place it in the slit between the paws.*

VARIATION: Color the squirrel red or brown if you have these colors on hand. You can make the nut out of construction paper.

HINT: Cardboard liners from panty hose work great for this craft.

Related Activities

1. ACTION VERSE:

Use your craft to provide the actions for this verse.

GRAY SQUIRREL, GRAY SQUIRREL,
WHISK YOUR BUSHY TAIL, (push tail back and forth)
WRINKLE UP YOUR FUNNY NOSE, (point to squirrel's nose)
HOLD A NUT BETWEEN YOUR TOES.

(place nut between squirrel's toes)

GRAY SQUIRREL, GRAY SQUIRREL,
WHISK YOUR BUSHY TAIL. (push tail back and forth)

2. VERSE:

THE SQUIRREL JUMPS FROM TREE TO TREE, (jump)
HE HIDES FROM YOU, HE HIDES FROM ME. (cover eyes)
HE LOOKS AND LOOKS, AND LOOKS AROUND,
(shade hand over eyes)
AND PICKS UP NUTS FROM OFF THE GROUND.
(bend down)

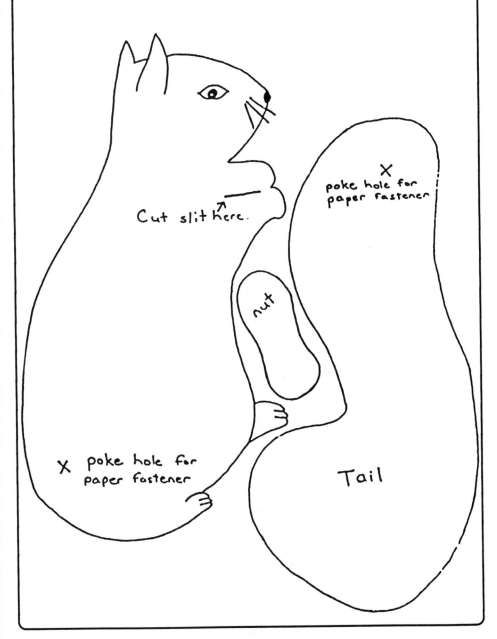

LION FACE

MATERIALS:
- Paper plates
- Pipe cleaners
- Black construction paper
- Black markers
- Crepe paper
- White glue
- Narrow elastic (or string)
- Scissors (or razor knife)

PREPARATION:
- *Cut two eyes out of each paper plate (see Diagram A). Save the eye shapes to be used as ears later. You may want to use a razor knife for this.*
- *Draw a triangle for the nose on each paper plate, and poke three holes on either side of each triangle (see Diagram B).*
- *Cut fringes for the manes from the crepe paper. Each fringe should be approx. 4" × 24" (10 cm × 60 cm) (see Diagram C).*
- *Cut triangles from black construction paper (see Diagram D).*

CHILD'S PLAY:
- *Place glue around the rim of the paper plate and stick on the mane (crepe paper fringe).*
- *Thread pipe cleaners through the holes in the triangles to create whiskers. Bend the ends of the pipe cleaners so they'll curl up.*
- *Glue black triangle on top of the whiskers to hide the holes and create a nose for your lion.*
- *Glue on ears (made from the eye shapes previously cut out).*
- *Draw a mouth for your lion with the black markers.*

Adult: *Poke holes in the side of each mask and tie on a piece of elastic 16" (40 cm) long so children can don the masks.*

Related Activities

1. SONG:

Sing to the tune of "London Bridge Is Falling Down."

> *I WENT TO VISIT THE ZOO ONE DAY,*
> *ZOO ONE DAY, ZOO ONE DAY,*
> *I SAW A LION ALONG THE WAY,*
> *AND THIS IS WHAT HE SAID TO ME . . .*
> > *ROAR! ROAR! ROAR!*

Repeat, naming different animals at the zoo, with their own unique sounds.

2. GAME: What Time Is It, Mr. Lion?

One child is appointed to be Mr. Lion, who sits on a chair with his back facing the rest of the children. The children ask the question "What time is it, Mr. Lion?" Mr. Lion replies by giving a time—"One o'clock" or "Two o'clock," for example. Eventually, however, he answers by saying "Dinner time!" The other children run while the lion tries to catch his dinner. The child who is caught becomes the next Mr. Lion.

Try to ensure that every child has a turn as Mr. Lion. When it's time to be Mr. Lion, each child will enjoy wearing the mask he or she made.

3. STORY TIME: "The Lion and the Mouse"
—Aesop's Fables

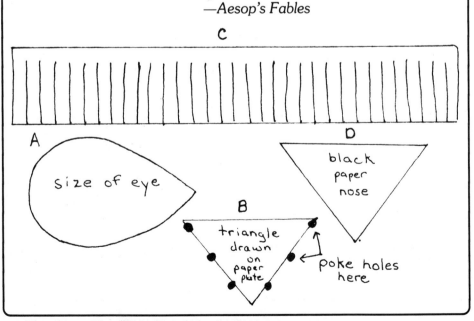

MY LITTLE DOG

MATERIALS:
- Large dog biscuits
- Cotton balls
- Brown felt
- White glue
- Scissors

PREPARATION:
- *Cut the shapes below out of brown felt.*

CHILD'S PLAY:
- *Glue ears to the top of the biscuit.*
- *Glue on eyes.*
- *Glue on white cotton ball.*
- *Glue brown felt nose to the cotton ball.*
- *Turn biscuit over and glue the tail to the bottom of the biscuit.*

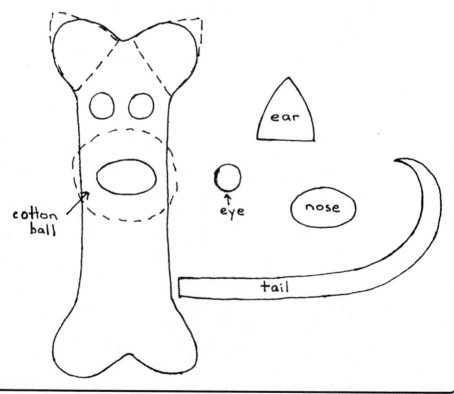

Related Activities

1. SONG:

OH WHERE, OH WHERE, HAS MY LITTLE DOG GONE?
OH WHERE, OH WHERE, CAN HE BE?
WITH HIS EARS CUT SHORT AND HIS TAIL CUT LONG,
OH WHERE, OH WHERE, CAN HE BE?

While children are singing this nursery rhyme, one child can close his or her eyes as another hides the little dog the first child made. Repeat until everyone has had a turn.

2. NURSERY RHYME:

HEY DIDDLE, DIDDLE, THE CAT AND THE FIDDLE,
THE COW JUMPED OVER THE MOON.
THE LITTLE DOG LAUGHED TO SEE SUCH A SIGHT,
AND THE DISH RAN AWAY WITH THE SPOON.

3. SIMPLE CRAFT:

Make a little doghouse by gluing six Popsicle sticks onto construction paper. First make a square with four sticks, then make a roof with the two remaining ones. Give your dog a name.

HINT: *The dog biscuit dog will fit inside the doghouse and can be glued in place if desired.*

ROBIN IN THE RAIN

MATERIALS:
- White paper
- Red tissue paper
- White glue
- Brushes for glue
- Brown crayons
- Blue paint
- Shallow container or containers

PREPARATION:
- *Trace the robin on white sheets of paper, one robin per child.*
- *Tear the red tissue paper into small pieces, approx. ½" (1 cm) square. (Older children can do this for themselves.)*
- *Place the blue paint in the shallow container.*

CHILD'S PLAY:
- *Brush the glue onto the robin's breast.*
- *Stick the little pieces of red tissue paper onto the glue.*
- *Use the brown crayon to draw the robin's wings, feet, and eye.*
- *Add any other additions you want. With your crayon you could draw a branch or worm, for example.*
- *Place your "pointer" finger in the blue paint and create drops of rain by pressing your finger onto the paper.*

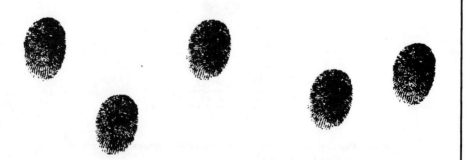

Related Activities

1. SONG:

Sing to the tune of "London Bridge Is Falling Down."

LITTLE ROBIN FLY BACK HERE,
FLY BACK HERE, FLY BACK HERE.
LITTLE ROBIN FLY BACK HERE,
NOW THAT SPRING IS COMING.

LITTLE ROBIN BUILD YOUR NEST...

LITTLE ROBIN SING YOUR SONG...

Continue this song, using suggestions from the children.

2. ACTION VERSE: *"Robin in the Nest"*

- *Children are in a squatting position.*
- *The children chant "Robin in the nest" three times, saying it louder each time.*
- *Give the children an opportunity to suggest their own ideas for this verse—e.g., robin in the tree, robin in the rain.*

HATCHING CHICKS

MATERIALS:

- Yellow powdered tempera
- Cotton balls
- Egg carton
- White glue
- Black and orange paper
- Self-stick circles (optional)
- Crayons (optional)
- Small paper bag
- One-hole punch (optional)
- Scissors
- Paper fasteners

PREPARATION:

- *For each child cut two sections from egg carton.*
- *Hinge the two sections together with a brass paper fastener.*
- *Place a couple of spoonfuls of yellow tempera in a small paper bag.*
- *Cut (or punch out) circles from the black paper for eyes. (If you have a one-hole punch, the children enjoy punching out their own circles.)*
- *Cut beaks from the orange paper.*

CHILD'S PLAY:

- *Drop two cotton balls into the bag with the yellow powder. Fold the bag down, and shake the bag.*
- *Take the cotton balls out of the bag and shake them over a garbage can.*
- *Glue one cotton ball to the inside of the "eggcup."*
- *Glue the other cotton ball on top of the first.*
- *Glue on eyes and beak.*
- *If you would like, decorate your egg with little self-stick circles or crayons.*
- *Now surprise someone by showing how your chick hatches (see related activity #4).*

Related Activities

1. FINGERPLAY:

FIVE EGGS AND FIVE EGGS, THAT MAKES TEN.

(hold up each hand in turn)

KEEPING THEM WARM IS THE MOTHER HEN.

(place one hand on top of the other)

CRACKLE, CRACKLE, POP, WHAT DO I SEE?

(wiggle fingers upward)

TEN LITTLE CHICKENS AS YELLOW AS CAN BE.

(hold up each hand)

2. SONG:

OLD McDONALD HAD A FARM,
  EE-IGH, EE-IGH, OH.
AND ON THAT FARM HE HAD SOME CHICKS,
  EE-IGH, EE-IGH, OH.
WITH A CHICK, CHICK HERE,
  AND A CHICK, CHICK THERE,
HERE A CHICK, THERE A CHICK,
  EVERYWHERE A CHICK, CHICK.
OLD McDONALD HAD A FARM,
  EE-IGH, EE-IGH, OH.

Repeat the verse with other animals suggested by the children.

3. STORY TIME: *"Chicken Little"*

Read or tell a version of this longtime favorite. I particularly enjoy the version in A Child's First Book of Nursery Tales, *which is edited by Selma Lanes and illustrated by Cyndy Szckeres.*

4. VERSE:

Demonstrate your craft with this verse:
  WHAT'S INSIDE THIS LITTLE EGG?
  IT'S FLUFFY AS CAN BE!
  WOULD YOU LIKE TO TAKE A GUESS?
  JUST OPEN IT UP AND SEE.
  PEEP! PEEP! PEEP! PEEP!

HERE'S A BUNNY

MATERIALS:
- Paper cups
- Popsicle sticks
- Glue
- Black crayon, white chalk
- Brown, pink, and green construction paper
- Scissors

PREPARATION:
- *Trace and cut out bunny heads on brown construction paper (see Diagram A). Provide one head per child.*
- *Trace and cut out the needed ear liners on pink construction paper (see Diagram B).*
- *Cut a fringe from green construction paper (see Diagram C).*

CHILD'S PLAY:
- *Glue pink ear liners onto the bunny's head.*
- *Bend each ear by folding it forward.*
- *Use the black crayon to draw the face.*
- *Draw the teeth by using white chalk.*
- *Glue the Popsicle stick to the back of the bunny.*
- *Glue the green fringe around the upper edge of the cup.*
- *Poke a hole in the bottom of the cup, and push the Popsicle stick through it so that the bunny head is sitting inside.*

Related Activities

1. VERSE: *"Here's a Bunny"*

HERE'S A BUNNY WITH EARS SO FUNNY,
AND HERE'S A HOLE IN THE GROUND;
AT THE FIRST SOUND HE HEARS,
HE PERKS UP HIS EARS,
AND POPS RIGHT INTO THE GROUND.

Use the craft to act out this verse.

2. SONG:

Sing to the tune of "London Bridge Is Falling Down."

LITTLE BUNNY CHANGE YOUR COAT,
CHANGE YOUR COAT,
    CHANGE YOUR COAT,
LITTLE BUNNY CHANGE YOUR COAT
NOW THAT SPRING IS COMING.

LITTLE BUNNY HOP AROUND . . .

3. GAME: *Hide & Seek*

You can play this game indoors or outdoors.
Someone is chosen to be mother bunny. Everyone
pretends to sleep at the beginning of the verse,
but at the third line the "baby bunnies" run and
hide. After about 10 seconds, the mother bunny
wakes up and tries to find her babies.

MOTHER BUNNY IS FAST ASLEEP,
BABIES MAKE NOT A PEEP,
BUT LITTLE BUNNIES LOVE TO PLAY,
SOFTLY NOW THEY HOP AWAY.

SPIDER ON THE WEB

MATERIALS:
- Black construction paper
- White paint
- Pipe cleaners, 12″ (30 cm) long
- Playdough (see recipe p. 53)
- Scissors

PREPARATION:
- *Cut some of the pipe cleaners into pieces approx. 4″ (10 cm) long. Provide four pieces per child.*
- *Twist one complete pipe cleaner around the middle of the smaller pieces to join them together.*
- *Twist another pipe cleaner to form a loop (handle) at one end.*

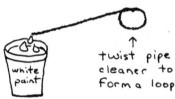

CHILD'S PLAY:
A.— *Hold on to the handle (loop) of your pipe cleaner and dip the end into white paint.*
- *Draw the pipe cleaner across the black paper, forming white streaks (spider's web).*
- *When you have enough streaks to form a spider's web, allow your paper to dry.*

B.— *Meanwhile, make a spider for your web by wrapping playdough around the center of the short pieces of pipe cleaner. Leave the ends of the pipe cleaners sticking out to form legs.*
- *Bend the pipe cleaners downward to give the legs shape.*
- *Set your spider on the web.*

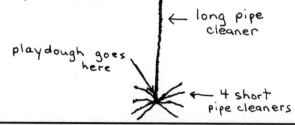

Related Activities

1. GAME: *Spider on the Web*

- *Children are in squatting position.*
- *The children chant "Spider on the web" three times, saying it louder each time.*
- *The fourth time, children say, "Spider out of the web" and jump up at the same time.*

Give the children an opportunity to suggest their own ideas for this verse.

2. NURSERY RHYME:

*LITTLE MISS MUFFET
SAT ON A TUFFET,
EATING HER CURDS AND WHEY;
ALONG CAME A SPIDER
WHO SAT DOWN BESIDE HER,
AND FRIGHTENED MISS MUFFET AWAY.*

Children love to dramatize this rhyme. One child is Miss Muffet while another child, using the spider he or she has made, frightens Miss Muffet away. If possible, all children should have an opportunity to act out both roles.

3. FINGERPLAY: *"Eency, Weency Spider"*

*EENCY, WEENCY SPIDER
WENT UP THE WATERSPOUT.
DOWN CAME THE RAIN
AND WASHED THE SPIDER OUT.
OUT CAME THE SUN
AND DRIED UP ALL THE RAIN,
SO THE EENCY, WEENCY SPIDER
WENT UP THE SPOUT AGAIN.*

4. SONG: *"Spider on the Floor"*

You will find this song in the book Singable Songs for the Very Young *by Raffi, with Ken Whiteley.*

The Warbler

From his tawny perch
high up in the pine,
he piped his own rendition
of some merry, little, praise tune—
And from his Jack Pine pulpit,
he opened drapes and windows,
and simply sang his sunlit song
for free!

Tine G. Buma

NATURE'S TREASURES

TURTLE "MAGNUT"

MATERIALS:

- Walnuts
- Green paint
- Paintbrushes
- Green felt
- White glue
- White chalk
- Magnetic strips
- Commercial eyes (optional)
- Nut-splitting tool, scissors

PREPARATION:

- *Split walnuts in half (I used a screwdriver to pry them open). Clean out the nuts.*
- *Trace turtle shape onto green felt and cut out the shape. Provide one per child.*
- *Draw the glue line on each piece of felt, using white chalk.*
- *Cut magnetic strips into pieces 1 inch (2 cm) long. Provide one strip per turtle shape.*

glue line

CHILD'S PLAY:

- *Paint the walnut shell green.*
- *Allow the paint to dry.*
- *Spread glue along the glue line on the green felt.*
- *Set your painted walnut on top of the glue.*
- *Glue eyes onto the turtle's head. (Black markers or little pieces of white felt can also be used to make eyes.)*
- *Peel adhesive off the magnetic strip and stick the strip on the underside of the turtle.*
- *Display your turtle on the fridge.*

HINT: Q-tips are great glue applicators.

Related Activities

1. FINGERPLAY: *"My Turtle"*

> ** HERE IS MY TURTLE,*
> *HE LIVES IN A SHELL,*
> *HIS HOME SUITS HIM VERY WELL;*
> ** HE POKES HIS HEAD OUT WHEN IT'S TIME TO EAT,*
> *AND HE PULLS IT BACK WHEN HE WANTS TO SLEEP.*

Children use their fists for shells and their thumbs for turtles. They extend their thumbs on the lines marked with an asterisk (*) and hide their thumbs in their fists on the other lines.

2. ACTION VERSE:

> *IF I WERE A TURTLE,*
> *SO VERY GREEN AND ROUND,*
> *I'D POKE MY LITTLE HEAD OUT,*
> *AND CRAWL ALONG THE GROUND.*

Children curl up in a ball on the floor. Then they poke their heads out and crawl along the ground.

3. COUNTING VERSE:

Display the children's turtles on a metallic surface. Stick a brown strip of paper beneath them to represent a log. Now have the children act out the following verse by taking their turtles off the "log" one at a time.

> *FIVE GREEN TURTLES ON A BUMPY LOG,*
> *SUNNING THEIR BACKS IN THE SWAMPY BOG,*
> *ONE TURTLE JUMPS IN THE WATER—WHEE!*
> *HOW MANY TURTLES ARE LEFT TO SEE?*
>
> *FOUR GREEN TURTLES . . .*

MILKWEED-POD BOAT

MATERIALS:
- Milkweed pods
- Playdough (plasticine or clay) (see recipe p. 53)
- Small twigs
- Paper squares, approx. 2" (5 cm) per side
- One-hole punch (optional)
- Crayons
- Scissors

PREPARATION:
- *Cut triangles out of the paper. Provide one triangle per child.*

CHILD'S PLAY:
- *Remove seeds from milkweed pod (see related activity #1).*
- *Put a small lump of playdough inside the milkweed pod.*
- *Print your initial on the triangle, or color an interesting design by using crayons.*
- *Punch a hole at the top and bottom of the triangular paper.*
- *Push your twig through the holes to form a sail.*
- *Press twig into playdough.*
- *You're ready to sail! Set you boat gently on top of a tub of water, and watch it float.*

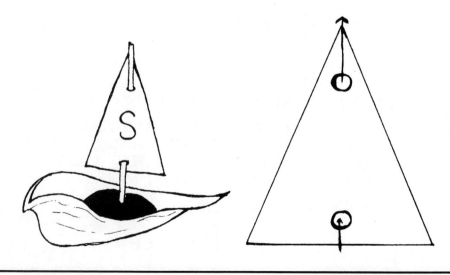

Related Activities

1. OUTDOOR FUN:

*IN A MILKWEED POD, COSY AND WARM,
LITTLE SEEDS ARE HIDING SAFE FROM HARM.
OPEN WIDE THE POD, AND HOLD IT UP HIGH,
COME ALONG WIND, HELP THE SEEDS FLY.*

Children love acting out this verse outdoors with an actual milkweed pod.

VARIATION: This verse can also be used as a fingerplay. For the first two lines, children close fingers into fists. For the third line, they slowly open up their fists and raise their hands in the air. Finally, they wiggle their fingers as the seeds fly away.

2. ACTION SONG:

Sing to the tune of "London Bridge Is Falling Down."

*FIVE LITTLE SEEDS, A-SLEEPING THEY LAY,
SLEEPING THEY LAY, SLEEPING THEY LAY,
A MOUSE CAME ALONG AND TOOK ONE AWAY,
HOW MANY SEEDS WERE LEFT THAT DAY?*

FOUR LITTLE SEEDS ...

Children pretend to be seeds sleeping on the floor. An adult can be the mouse and take one child away. Continue the song until the "mouse" has taken all the "seeds" away.

3. FINGERPLAY:

*FIVE LITTLE SEEDS IN A MILKPOD PRESSED,
ONE GREW, TWO GREW, AND SO DID ALL THE REST.
THEY GREW AND GREW, AND DID NOT STOP,
UNTIL ONE DAY THE POD WENT "POP."*

(clap hands together)

SUNFLOWERS

MATERIALS:
- Sunflower seeds (in shells)
- Paper cups
- Yellow paint
- Paintbrushes
- Glue
- Green construction paper
- Tape
- Scissors
- Brushes for glue

PREPARATION:
- *Cut a long strip of construction paper for a stem. Allow one stem per child.*
- *Put a few drops of yellow paint into a cup, one cup for each child.*

CHILD'S PLAY:
- *With your paintbrush, smear the paint around the inside of the cup until the inside is covered in brilliant yellow.*
- *Set the cup on its side and allow the paint to dry. (Meanwhile, try the related activities.)*
- *Make several cuts from the rim to the base of the cup.*
- *Press down on cut strips to form open petals.*
- *Brush glue on the center of flower (inside bottom of cup).*
- *Press sunflower seeds onto the glue.*
- *Allow glue to dry.*
- *Tape green strip of paper to the back of flower.*
- *Display sunflowers in a row.*

Related Activities

1. SONG:

Sing to the tune of "One Little, Two Little, Three Little Indians."

ONE LITTLE, TWO LITTLE,
*   THREE LITTLE SUNFLOWERS,*
FOUR LITTLE, FIVE LITTLE,
*   SIX LITTLE SUNFLOWERS,*
SEVEN LITTLE, EIGHT LITTLE,
*   NINE LITTLE SUNFLOWERS,*
TEN LITTLE SUNFLOWERS IN A ROW.

On a bulletin board or wall, display the sunflowers the children have made. Use this song to count the flowers.

2. TASTY TREAT:

This treat is both nutritious and delicious—a wonderful combination. Children love to help make these tasty snacks.

1 cup (250 ml) Cheerios
1/3 cup (80 ml) hulled sunflower seeds
1/3 cup (80 ml) peanut butter at room temperature
1/4 cup (60 ml) raisins
2 tbsp. (30 ml) honey
1 tbsp. (15 ml) milk

- *Pour all ingredients into a large bowl.*
- *Mix with a tablespoon until completely blended.*
- *Roll mixture into balls.*
- *Refrigerate balls in airtight containers.*

3. ACTION VERSE:

BEND AND STRETCH, REACH FOR THE SKY,
TALL AS A SUNFLOWER, YOU AND I.
BEND AND STRETCH, NOW NOD YOUR HEAD,
SPREAD OUT YOUR SEEDS,
SO THE BIRDS CAN BE FED.

The children do the actions described in the first three lines. On the fourth line, children sway their arms back and forth above their heads.

FOOTPRINTS
IN THE SAND

MATERIALS:

- Sand
- Construction paper
  (in a color to contrast with paint)
- Tempera paint
- Shallow container or containers

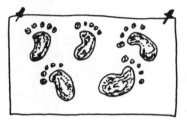

PREPARATION:

- *Pour paint in shallow container or containers. (We used bright yellow paint and black construction paper.)*

CHILD'S PLAY:

- *Dip the side of your fist into the paint and press it onto the paper. You should be able to make a couple of prints before dipping your fist into the paint again.*
- *Now dip your fingers and thumb in the paint.*
- *Keep your fingers close together and press down on the paper, in front of fist print, to create "toes."*
- *Repeat until you have covered your paper with prints.*
- *Sprinkle sand over the wet paint.*
- *Shake off the excess sand, and you will be left with "footprints in the sand."*

Related Activities

1. ACTION VERSE:

FIRST YOU WALK UPON YOUR TOES,
THEN DOWN ON HEELS YOU MUST GO,
NOW ON SIDES OF YOUR FEET GO
                    —CLUMP, CLUMP, CLUMP,
AND WITH YOUR FEET TOGETHER GO
                    —JUMP, JUMP, JUMP!

2. SONG:

Sing to the tune of "London Bridge Is Falling Down." Set out cardboard squares or small pieces of carpet, to represent stepping-stones. The children, barefooted, act out this song as they step from one stone to the next:

STEPPING ACROSS STEPPING-STONES,
STEPPING-STONES, STEPPING-STONES,
STEPPING ACROSS STEPPING-STONES,
ONE, TWO, THREE!

THE RIVER IS VERY FAST AND WIDE,
FAST AND WIDE, FAST AND WIDE,
THE RIVER IS VERY FAST AND WIDE,
COME WITH ME!

3. OUTDOOR FUN:

You need two tubs, one with tempera paint covering the bottom and the other filled with soapy water, and a roll of wallpaper approx. 3 yards (3 meters) long. Spread out the paper (plain side up) and hold it down at each end with one of the tubs. The barefooted children take turns stepping into the tub of paint, walking the length of the paper, and then stepping into the tub of soapy water.

STARRY NIGHT

MATERIALS:

- Apples
- Black construction paper
- White tempera paint
- Paper towels
- Shallow containers
  (meat trays work well)
- Knife
- Star cookie cutter (optional)

PREPARATION:

NOTE: *Do related activity #1 before starting this craft. Children can munch on apple pieces while watching you carve the apples.*

- *Cut apples in half, crosswise (not stem to blossom). Provide one apple half per child.*
- *Remove seeds and wipe off the cut surfaces.*
- *Press cookie cutter into the cut surface of each apple and carve around it with knife. (If you don't have a cookie cutter, carve your own star shape.)*
- *Fold paper towels into quarters and place them in the shallow containers.*
- *Pour tempera paint onto the paper towels.*

CHILD'S PLAY:

- *Dip your "apple star" (cut surface) in the paint.*
- *Press apple on the black construction paper —you can press your apple down a few times before you'll need to dip into the paint again.*
- *Cover your paper with star prints.*

HINT: *Older children may want to make constellations such as the Big Dipper.*

Related Activities

1. ACTIVITY POEM:

Children will be all eyes when you demonstrate this poem with an apple and knife.

HERE'S AN APPLE AS RED AS IT CAN BE,
DID YOU KNOW THERE'S A SECRET INSIDE
JUST WAITING FOR YOU AND ME?
WE'LL TAKE A KNIFE AND CUT IT IN TWO,
AND THERE'S A LITTLE STAR TWINKLING AT YOU.

2. NURSERY RHYME:

TWINKLE, TWINKLE, LITTLE STAR,
HOW I WONDER WHAT YOU ARE.
UP ABOVE THE WORLD SO HIGH,
LIKE A DIAMOND IN THE SKY.

3. PLAYDOUGH FUN:

Follow recipe for playdough on p. 53. Make star shapes, using yellow or white playdough and cookie cutters. Arrange your stars on black construction paper and form different "pictures in the sky."

4. ACTION SONG:

BEND AND STRETCH, REACH FOR THE SKY
STAND ON TIPPY TOES, WAY UP HIGH

(hands overhead)

BEND AND STRETCH, REACH FOR THE STARS,
THERE GOES JUPITER, HERE COMES MARS.

(hands overhead, moving from one side to the other)

5. SNACK TIME: *"Happy Apple"*

HAPPY APPLE IS GOOD AND SWEET.
HAPPY APPLE IS NICE TO EAT.
HAPPY APPLE WAS CUT IN TWO.
HALF FOR ME AND HALF FOR YOU.

THE ACORN MAN

MATERIALS:
- Acorn caps
- Oak leaves
- White paper
- Brown construction paper
- Glue
- Tempera paint
- Paintbrushes
- Newspaper
- Crayons
- Scissors

PREPARATION:
- *Cut the acorn shapes from the brown paper (see Diagrams A and B). If you have two different shades of brown, use the darker shade for the cap.*
- *Set oak leaves on a sheet of newspaper, providing one leaf per child. Put another sheet of newspaper at each child's place.*

CHILD'S PLAY:
- *Brush paint (choose a bright color) over the entire surface of the leaf.*
- *Set the painted leaf on the clean sheet of newspaper. Place the leaf near the bottom of the page so you have room to add the head.*
- *Lay white paper over top of the leaf.*
- *Rub paper with clean, dry hands.*
- *Turn paper over and carefully remove leaf.*
- *Glue actual acorn caps to the brown acorn shape, to create eyes and nose.*
- *Draw in a mouth with crayon.*
- *Glue acorn head to white paper at top of leaf print.*

OPTIONAL: *If you wish, use your crayons to add feet and hands or any other features you might like.*

Related Activities

1. SONG:

Sing to the tune "Oh, Do You Know the Muffin Man?"

OH, DO YOU KNOW THE ACORN MAN,
THE ACORN MAN, THE ACORN MAN?
OH, DO YOU KNOW THE ACORN MAN,
WHO LIVES UNDER THE OLD OAK TREE?

OH, YES, I KNOW THE ACORN MAN...

2. PLAYDOUGH IMPRESSIONS:

See the playdough recipe, p. 53.
Have fun with acorns and playdough. Suggestions:
a) Press the acorn caps into the playdough. What shape do they leave behind?
b) Form a ball of playdough and create funny faces by sticking in the acorn nuts and caps for eyes, nose, etc.

3. ACTION VERSE:

At the beginning of the verse, the children are in a squatting position. Gradually they stand up with arms out wide and finally up on "tippy toes."

IF YOU WERE AN OAK TREE,
WHAT WOULD YOU DO?
I'D GROW AND GROW AND GROW SO HIGH,
UNTIL I ALMOST REACHED THE SKY!

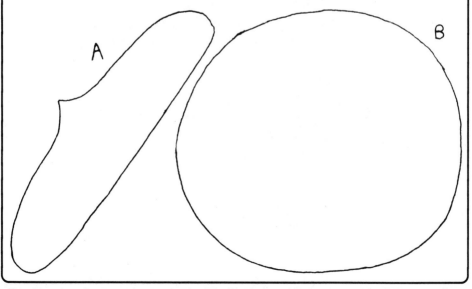

PINECONE FEEDER

MATERIALS:

- Large pinecones
- Popcorn
- Raisins
- Red paint
- Paintbrushes
- Pieces of string
  each approx. 7″ (18 cm) long

PREPARATION:

- *Pop the popcorn.*

CHILD'S PLAY:

- *Paint the scales of the pinecones red.*
- *Let the paint dry. (Try the related activities.)*
- *Gently but firmly place kernels of popcorn, one at a time, up and under the scales.*
- *Place raisins under the scales around the top section of the cone.*
- *Tie a string around the top of the pinecone feeder.*
- *Hang the cone from a tree that's visible from a window, and watch the birds enjoy a winter treat.*

Related Activities

1. SONG:

Sing to the tune "Baa, Baa, Black Sheep"

I FOUND A PINECONE, LOOK AT ME,
I FOUND A PINECONE, UNDER THE TREE.
LOOK ON THE INSIDE, WHAT DO YOU SEE?
A TINY SEED THAT WILL MAKE A PINE TREE.

I FOUND A PINECONE, LOOK AT ME,
I FOUND A PINECONE, UNDER THE TREE.

2. SIMPLE BIRD FEEDERS:

You need a few pieces of stale bread (to make my bread stale, I left it out on the counter overnight) and some cookie cutters. Cutters in the shapes of trees, stars, and the like work especially well. Press the cutters into the bread to form the shapes. Poke a hole near the top of each shape, then thread a string through each hole. Tie the shapes to your favorite tree so the birds can enjoy the feeders you've made.

3. PINECONE DECORATION:

Simple to make—pretty to see!

Gradually add approx. 1/4 cup (60 ml) hot water to 1 cup (250 ml) of Ivory Soap flakes and beat with a mixer until stiff. Use your fingers to place the soap mixture on the scales of the pinecone to resemble snow. Then sprinkle glitter over top of the soap and shake off the excess. Tie a string to the top of the pinecone and suspend it from a Christmas tree.

OH, CHRISTMAS TREE

MATERIALS:
- Pine branches
- White paper
- Green paint
- Paper clips
- Crayons
- Glitter and glue
- Small circle stickers (optional)
- Scissors

PREPARATION:
- *Cut a tree frame out of the white paper (see Diagram A).*
- *Fasten the tree frame to another sheet of white paper by using paper clips (see Diagram B).*

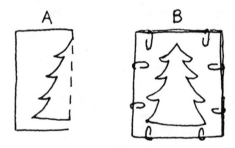

CHILD'S PLAY:
- *Dip the pine branch in the green paint, and with vertical strokes brush it over the tree frame.*
- *Cover the entire frame with paint.*
- *Remove the paper clips and lift off the frame—magically a beautiful tree appears!*
- *Allow tree to dry.*
- *Decorate with crayons, glitter and glue, and stickers to transform the painted tree into a Christmas tree. Some of the things you can add include presents, ornaments, tinsel, and a star.*

HINT: *If you happen to have an easel, it's ideal for this craft.*

Related Activities

1. ACTION SONG:

Sing to the tune of "I'm a Little Teapot."

I'M A LITTLE PINE TREE, WITH BRANCHES GREEN.
(hold arms out to side)

YOU CAN DECORATE ME TO MAKE A CHRISTMAS SCENE.
(sway from side to side)

DON'T FORGET TO PUT THE STAR ON TOP;
(point to the top of head)

BE VERY CAREFUL SO THE BALLS DON'T DROP.
(sway from side to side)

2. OUTDOOR FUN:

Go for a walk to identify pine trees in your neighborhood. If you do this before doing the craft Oh, Christmas Tree, children can find their own branches to paint with.

3. SIMPLE CRAFT:

- *Children can color the leftover tree shapes cut out from the frames.*
- *Cut a slit in one tree from the bottom to halfway up the tree.*
- *Cut a slit in a second tree from the top to halfway down the tree.*
- *Interlock slits to create a three-dimensional tree.*

4. SONG:

Sing to the tune "Here We Go 'Round the Mulberry Bush."

HERE STANDS A BRIGHT GREEN CHRISTMAS TREE, CHRISTMAS TREE, CHRISTMAS TREE. HERE STANDS A BRIGHT GREEN CHRISTMAS TREE, SO EARLY IN THE MORNING.

HERE ARE LIGHTS SHINING SO BRIGHT . . .

HERE ARE PRESENTS FOR ONE AND ALL . . .

CELEBRATION TREE

MATERIALS:
- Branch
- Playdough (see recipe p. 53)
- Medium flowerpot
- Tape
- Glue
- Felt
- Scissors

PREPARATION:
- Go for a walk and find a branch with lots of twigs. (Lilac trees are ideal!)
- Cut a rectangle of felt, large enough to fit around the flowerpot. If necessary, cut shapes from felt (see related activity #1).

CHILD'S PLAY:
- Fill flowerpot with playdough.
- Poke branch into the center of playdough.
- Press playdough firmly around the branch to hold it in place.
- Tape felt to pot. Using tape instead of glue ensures easy removal for the next celebration.
- Decorate felt and tree according to the celebration. (See related activity #1 for suggestions.)

Related Activities

1. CELEBRATION TREE:

Suggestions:

OCCASION	TREE DECORATION	POT DECORATION
Valentine's Day	● *recycled hearts, p. 90*	● *red felt/pink hearts*
St. Patrick's Day	● *St. Patrick pendants, p. 52*	● *dark green felt/light green shamrocks*
Easter	● *painted blown eggs*	● *blue felt/yellow chicks*
Autumn	● *waxed leaves*	● *felt in fall colors*
Halloween	● *pumpkin faces*	● *black felt/orange jack-o-lanterns*
Christmas	● *pinecone decoration, p. 47* ● *dough shapes* ● *candy canes, etc.*	● *red felt/evergreen trees*

2. COUNTING VERSE:

Once the children have decorated the celebration tree, they can act out this verse by removing their craft from the tree, one at a time.

FIVE LITTLE _____ ON THE TREE,
ONE FOR YOU AND ONE FOR ME.
TAKE ONE _____ OFF THE TREE,
HOW MANY _____ DO YOU SEE?

FOUR LITTLE _____ . . .

For each underscore, substitute the name of the craft to be removed.

3. BARK RUBBINGS:

All you need is thin paper, dark crayons (with paper removed), and masking tape. Tape the paper to a tree trunk and rub hard with the side of the crayon. Try different trees and note the variation in the rubbings. To dress up the picture, tape or glue it onto cardboard and add a frame made out of construction paper.

ST. PATRICK PENDANT

MATERIALS:
- Clover
- Green playdough
- Drinking straw
- Yarn
- Shamrock or clover cookie cutter
- Scissors

PREPARATION:
- *Use green food coloring to make playdough. Follow recipe on p. 53.*
- *Cut straw into small pieces, each approx. 3/4" (2 cm) long.*
- *Cut yarn into lengths of approx. 20" (50 cm) each.*
- *Take the children on a clover hunt. If you look carefully in the patches of grass, you will find clover. Spring is just around the corner!*

CHILD'S PLAY:
- *Flatten playdough with your hands or a rolling pin until the dough is approx. 1/4" (5 mm) thick.*
- *Cut out a shamrock shape by using a shamrock or clover cookie cutter.*
- *Poke a piece of straw into top of shamrock.*
- *Gently press clover leaf into center of shamrock.*
- *Let shamrock dry overnight, then remove straw and clover leaf.*
- *String shamrock on yarn and wear it as a pendant.*

HINT: **Cut the shamrock shape on a piece of cardboard to make the dough portable while drying.**

Related Activities

1. SHAMROCK PRINTS:

Press a shamrock cookie cutter onto an ink pad and then press the cutter onto a piece of paper. Repeat several times until your paper is covered in shamrock prints. Color or paint the shamrocks green.

2. ST. PATRICK'S DAY LEGEND:

March 17 honors the patron saint of Ireland, St. Patrick. Legend has it that St. Patrick used the shamrock to illustrate the idea of the Trinity.

- Cut three, equal-sized hearts out of green construction paper.
- Poke a hole in the bottom of each heart.
- Join hearts together by putting a paper fastener through the holes.
- The hearts can be held up as one or separated to form a shamrock—three in one!

3. PLAYDOUGH RECIPE:

Dry: (Mix in medium pan)
2 cups (500 ml) flour
1 cup (250 ml) salt
4 tsp. (20 ml) cream of tartar

Wet: (Mix together)
2 cups (500 ml) water
2 tbsp. (30 ml) cooking oil
1 tsp. (5 ml) food coloring

- Add wet ingredients to dry ingredients.
- Cook 3 to 5 minutes over medium heat, stirring constantly.
- Knead until smooth.
- KEEP IN AN AIRTIGHT CONTAINER UNTIL READY TO USE.

BIRD'S NEST

MATERIALS:
- Hard-boiled white and/or brown eggs
- Cardboard
- White glue
- Paintbrushes
- Construction paper
- Crayons or markers
- Masking tape (optional)
- Brushes for glue

PREPARATION:
- *Provide at least as many hard-boiled eggs as there are children. (I used a combination of brown and white eggs to produce a speckled look.)*
- *Peel off eggshells and rinse them. Set them aside to dry, and then crush them.*
- *Refrigerate the eggs to use later for snack time.*
- *Cut four or five egg shapes per child, from the cardboard.*
- *Draw nest—approx. 5 1/2" (14 cm) wide—on construction paper.*

CHILD'S PLAY:
- *Brush one of the paper eggs with glue and sprinkle on eggshells.*
- *Repeat until all the paper eggs are covered with eggshells.*
- *Shake off excess eggshells.*
- *Color your nest.*
- *Glue eggs in the nest.*
- *Add any other details with your crayons. You could draw a bird, branch, leaves, etc.*

VARIATION:
Use dried moss for a nest. Moss glues easily on the paper.

HINT: **Put masking tape on the back of the eggs and secure them to the newspaper. This way they won't move around when you brush on the glue.**

Related Activities

1. ACTION VERSE: *"Bird in the Egg"*

- *Children are in squatting position.*
- *They chant "Bird in the egg" three times, saying it louder each time.*
- *The fourth time, the children say "Bird out of the egg" and jump up at the same time.*
- *Give the children an opportunity to suggest their own ideas for this verse—e.g., bird in the nest.*

2. SNACK TIME:

"Egg Faces"

Set hard-boiled eggs in an eggcup. For each child provide toothpicks and small edibles: Cheerios (with raisins stuffed in their centers), cheese, popcorn, grapes, dried fruit, cooked macaroni, and mini-marshmallows. Children can create their own egg faces and then enjoy a delicious snack.

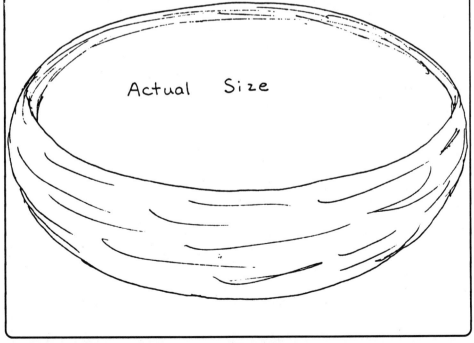

Actual Size

PUSSY WILLOW

MATERIALS:
- Pussy willows
- Black construction paper
- White glue
- White chalk
- Blue crayon or paper

PREPARATION:
- *Remove the pussy-willow flowers (catkins) from the twigs. You need lots.*
- *Use the chalk to draw the kitten shape on the black construction paper. Provide one shape per child.*
- *Just before children are ready to do the craft, squeeze white glue along the kitten outline. (Older children can do this on their own.)*

CHILD'S PLAY:
- *Place catkins along the glue line.*
- *Draw blue eyes, or glue on two blue paper circles.*
- *Draw in whiskers with white chalk.*
- *Lay the cardboard flat so it can dry.*

Related Activities

1. NURSERY RHYME:

PUSSY CAT, PUSSY CAT, WHERE HAVE YOU BEEN?
I'VE BEEN TO LONDON TO VISIT THE QUEEN.
PUSSY CAT, PUSSY CAT, WHAT DID YOU THERE?
I FRIGHTENED A LITTLE MOUSE UNDER HER CHAIR!

An adult can ask the question in lines 1 and 3. The children respond in lines 2 and 4 while holding up the pussy cat they made.

2. GAME: *"Nice Kitty"*

One child is chosen to be the kitty. The rest of the children sit in a circle. The kitty goes to each child in turn, and each pets the kitty, saying "Nice kitty"; the kitty makes no reply. Finally, the kitty responds to one child by meowing. That child must run around the outside of the circle, with the kitty in pursuit. If the child can return to his or her place without being caught by the kitty, that child becomes the new kitty.

3. SONG: *"Pussy Willow"*

I HAVE A LITTLE PUSSY
HER COAT IS SILVER GRAY
SHE LIVES DOWN IN THE MEADOW
NOT VERY FAR AWAY
SHE'LL ALWAYS BE A PUSSY
SHE'LL NEVER BE A CAT
CAUSE SHE'S A PUSSY WILLOW
NOW WHAT DO YOU THINK OF THAT!
MEOW, MEOW, MEOW, MEOW, MEOW,
MEOW, . . . SCAT!

BLOSSOM TIME

MATERIALS:

- Popcorn
- Brown crayons
- White construction paper
- Powdered tempera, red
- Medium-sized paper bag
- White glue
- Q-Tips

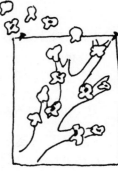

PREPARATION:

- *Draw a branch on construction paper (see the diagram to the right). Older children can draw their own branches.*
- *Put 2 tsp. (10 ml) of red powdered tempera in the paper bag.*
- *Add 3 cups (750 ml) of popcorn and shake to produce pink "blossoms."*

CHILD'S PLAY:

- *Color the branch brown.*
- *Using a Q-Tip, put a spot of glue on the branch. (Don't skimp on glue.)*
- *Press popcorn, gently but firmly, onto glue.*
- *Repeat this process until branch is covered in blossoms.*
- *Lay picture flat to dry.*

Related Activities

1. VERSE:

IT'S MAY TIME, IT'S BLOSSOM TIME,
THERE ARE FLOWERS ON THE TREES,
A HAPPY TIME FOR CHILDREN,
AND A BUSY TIME FOR BEES.

2. SNACK TIME: *Caramel Corn*

Melt 1/4 lb. (115 g) caramel candy and 2 tbsp. (30 ml) water in the top of a double boiler. When the mixture makes a smooth sauce, pour it over 2 quarts (2 l) of salted popcorn. Stir until evenly mixed. Spread on a lightly buttered cookie sheet to cool. Break the caramel corn into small chunks to eat.

NATURE PIÑATA

MATERIALS:

- Round balloon
- Newspaper
- Shallow dishes or pans
- Glue
- Paintbrushes
- Brushes for glue
- Natural materials—e.g., leaves, wildflowers, etc.
- Treats—e.g., boxes of raisins, candies, party favors

PREPARATION:

- *Blow up balloon.*
- *Rip newspapers into strips of approx. 1" × 3" (2.5 cm × 7.5 cm).*

CHILD'S PLAY:

- *Soak some of the newspaper strips in a shallow dish of water.*
- *Cover the balloon with these wet strips. (Leave the area around balloon stem clear.)*
- *Soak the remaining newspaper strips in a mixture of half glue, half water.*
- *Cover the balloon with these sticky strips. (Two layers are preferable.)*
- *Let dry overnight.*
- *Pop the balloon and remove it through the opening where the balloon stem was.*
- *Brush glue on the piñata and stick on the natural materials— the leaves, wildflowers, etc.*
- *Fill piñata with treats by dropping them through the opening.*
- *Cover opening with a large leaf.*
- *Suspend the piñata from a tree branch. (Suggestions: Use a plant hanger or run some string up through the middle of the piñata so it comes out the top.)*
- *Find a sturdy stick, and take turns hitting the piñata until the treats spill out.*

Related Activities

1. SONG:

Sing to the tune of "Goodnight, Ladies."

> *HELLO SPRING, HELLO SPRING,*
> *HELLO SPRING, WE'RE GLAD TO SEE YOU HERE!*

> *HELLO LEAVES...*

> *HELLO PUSSY WILLOWS...*

> *HELLO FLOWERS...*

Continue, using ideas the children suggest.

2. OUTDOOR FUN:

Go for a hike in the woods or even in your own neighborhood and look for signs of spring. For example:

- *Buds on the trees*
- *Crocuses*
- *Pussy willows*

3. SPRING DISPLAY:

Set aside a bulletin board or wall for a spring display and add a new craft to it every week (or every day if you're ambitious). Start with a border of grass at the bottom, then add the following:

1. *Robin in the Rain, p. 24*
2. *Blossom Time, p. 58*
3. *Branches decorated with yellow tissue paper*
4. *Pussy Willow, p. 56*
5. *Daffodil, Daffodil, p. 78*
6. *Fanciful Butterfly, p. 10*
7. *Sunflowers, p. 38*

Fingerpainted sheets of paper can be cut to shapes, such as clouds and the sun, to add the finishing touches to your display.

Art is man's nature;
nature is God's art.

P. J. Bailey

UNDERSTANDING
NATURE

WIND SOCK

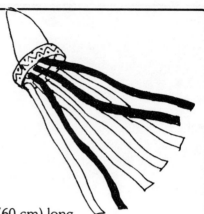

MATERIALS:
- Crepe paper (different colors)
- Cardboard
- Glue
- One-hole punch
- Stapler
- Crayons
- String cut in pieces approx. 24" (60 cm) long
- Flat stone (optional)
- Scissors

PREPARATION:
- *Cut strips of different colors of crepe paper. Each strip should be approx. 1" × 20" (3 cm × 50 cm). Provide 10 strips per wind sock.*
- *Cut a cardboard strip that is approx. 1½" × 16" (4 cm × 40 cm). Provide one strip per wind sock.*

CHILD'S PLAY:
- *Draw a design on the cardboard strip by using crayons.*
- *Turn cardboard over and glue on strips of crepe paper in a row.*

Adult: *This is a great opportunity to encourage sequencing— e.g., red, yellow, blue, red, yellow, etc.*

- *Staple the ends of the cardboard strip together to form a circle. (Crepe strips should be on the inside of circle and crayon design on the outside.)*
- *Punch a hole on either side of the cardboard circle and tie on the string.*
- *Take your wind sock outside and see which direction the wind is blowing.*

OPTIONAL: *You can glue a weight, such as a flat stone, to the inside of the cardboard. This ensures that the mouth of the wind sock faces into the wind. The only drawback is that you have to let the glue dry before taking your wind sock outdoors.*

Related Activities

1. SONG:

Sing to the tune of "Did You Ever See a Lassie?"

*DID YOU EVER SEE THE WIND BLOW,
THE WIND BLOW, THE WIND BLOW,
DID YOU EVER SEE THE WIND BLOWING
THIS WAY AND THAT?
THIS WAY AND THAT WAY, THIS WAY AND
    THAT WAY,
DID YOU EVER SEE THE WIND BLOWING
THIS WAY AND THAT?*

Children sway back and forth while singing "This way and that."

2. ACTION VERSE: *"Windy Days"*

*LIKE A LEAF OR FEATHER
IN THE WINDY, WINDY WEATHER,
WE WHIRL ABOUT AND TWIRL ABOUT
AND ALL SINK DOWN TOGETHER.*

3. WINDY DAY FUN:

Put a couple of spoonfuls of paint on white drawing paper. Go outside and hold your paper up into the wind. Watch the designs the wind creates on your paper.

4. STORY TIME: *Gilberto and the Wind*
by M. H. Ets

This is one of my all-time favorite books.

BUBBLE PRINTS

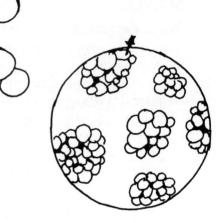

MATERIALS:
- Tempera paint
- Liquid dishwashing detergent
- Water
- Straws
- Paper plates
- Cups (or paint pots)
- Pin

PREPARATION:
- *Mix 1 tbsp. (15 ml) paint and 1 tbsp. (15 ml) liquid detergent together in each cup or paint pot. Add 1/4 cup (60 ml) water and stir. If you want different colors, make a separate cup of solution for each one. Provide one container of mixture per child.*
- *Use a pin to poke a couple of holes near the top of each straw to prevent children from sucking in the mixture.*

CHILD'S PLAY:
- *Place your straw in the solution and blow to create a mound of bubbles.*
- *Slowly lower the paper plate onto the bubbles, and a beautiful design will appear. (Be careful to just touch the bubbles and not the container.)*
- *Repeat this procedure until your paper plate is covered in bubble designs. We used different colors—the children exchanged their cups.*

HINT: *Keep a cloth handy to wipe off the ends of the straws when children change colors. Spillproof paint pots are great for making bubble prints.*

Related Activities

1. OUTDOOR FUN:

- *Mix 1/4 cup (60 ml) of liquid dishwashing detergent with 1 cup (250 ml) of water.*
- *Twist pipe cleaners to form a circle at one end, creating a wand. Now you're ready for some soap bubble magic.*
- *Dip wand in bubble mixture and slowly wave it through the air.*
- *Dip wand again and wave it quickly through the air.*
- *Try blowing softly into the wand.*
- *Blow hard into the wand.*
  (Help the children draw the conclusion that slow-moving air makes a few large bubbles and fast-moving air makes many small bubbles.)
- *Catch a bubble on your wand and look through it at a friend.*
- *What happens when you try to catch a bubble with your hand? Put a little detergent on your hand and see what happens.*
- *Twist the pipe cleaners into figure eights or other shapes and see what kind of bubbles you can create.*

2. SONG:

Sing to the tune of "Here We Go 'Round the Mulberry Bush."

> *THIS IS THE WAY WE BLOW OUR BUBBLES,*
> *BLOW OUR BUBBLES, BLOW OUR BUBBLES,*
> *THIS IS THE WAY WE BLOW OUR BUBBLES*
>
> (children blow air from their mouths, 3 times)
>
> *THIS IS THE WAY WE BREAK OUR BUBBLES,*
> *BREAK OUR BUBBLES, BREAK OUR BUBBLES,*
> *THIS IS THE WAY WE BREAK OUR BUBBLES*
>
> (children clap their hands, 3 times)

SUN HAT

MATERIALS:
- Bristol board (or cardboard)
- Yellow crepe paper (or tissue paper)
- Yellow paint
- Paintbrushes
- Yarn
- Stapler
- Scissors

PREPARATION:
- *Cut a circle from the bristol board. The diameter of the circle should be approx. 13" (32 cm).*
- *Cut out a quarter of the circle. (You can fold the circle twice to show exactly where to cut.)*
- *Cut crepe paper into small rectangles of approx. 1" × 3" (2 cm × 6 cm) each.*

CHILD'S PLAY:
- *Use yellow paint to paint the bristol board shape.*
- *Stick the crepe paper rectangles onto the yellow paint while it's still wet—especially around the rim to create a little fringe (which will resemble sun's rays).*
- *Allow paint to dry.*
- *With the help of an adult, staple the cut edges of the shape together to form a hat.*
- *Poke a hole on either side of the hat and, to each side, tie on a piece of yarn approx. 15" (40 cm).*
- *Now try your sun hat on for size.*

Related Activities

1. SONG: *"Mr. Sun"*

OH MR. SUN, SUN, MR. GOLDEN SUN,
PLEASE SHINE DOWN ON ME.
OH MR. SUN, SUN, MR. GOLDEN SUN,
HIDING BEHIND A TREE.
THESE LITTLE CHILDREN ARE ASKING YOU
TO PLEASE COME OUT SO WE CAN PLAY WITH YOU.
OH MR. SUN, SUN, MR. GOLDEN SUN,
PLEASE SHINE DOWN ON ME.

2. GAME:

* *SALLY GO ROUND THE SUN,*
   SALLY GO ROUND THE MOON,
   SALLY GO ROUND THE CHIMNEY TOPS,
   EVERY AFTERNOON. BOOM!

* *Substitute names of the children in your group.*

One child is chosen to be the sun and stands in the center of a circle made by the rest of the children. The child who is the sun wears his or her sun hat while the others skip around saying "Sally go round the sun . . . " When they come to "Boom!" they all fall down. Repeat until everyone has had a turn being the sun.

3. EXPERIMENT:

- *Plant a few bean seeds in two containers (see p. 80).*
- *Put one container in a sunny spot and one in the dark.*
- *Sprinkle with water daily.*
- *After beans sprout, continue to water for a couple of weeks.*
- *Observe the difference in growth.*
- *Conclusions: BEANS NEED THE SUN!*
                WE NEED THE SUN!

I CAN MAKE A RAINBOW

MATERIALS:
- Construction paper
- Crayons in rainbow colors
- Yarn in rainbow colors
- Crepe paper in rainbow colors
- Glue
- Spray bottle
- Scissors

PREPARATION:
- *Draw four arcs on the construction paper with the china markers. (We used red, yellow, green, and blue. Check the guide below for actual rainbow colors.)*
- *Cut yarn the same length as the arcs.*
- *Cut crepe paper into rectangles of approx. 1" × 3" (2 cm × 7 cm).*

CHILD'S PLAY:
- *After an adult places glue on the arcs, stick yarn on top (red, yellow, green, blue).*
- *Put rectangles of red crepe paper in the arc below the red yarn, yellow paper below yellow yarn, etc. until every arc is filled with crepe paper.*
- *Spray your rainbow with water from the spray bottle.*
- *Once the crepe paper is soaked with water, slowly pull it off. It magically leaves a rainbow of colors.*
- *Hang your rainbow in a window and you will be able to see it indoors and out.*

VARIATION:
> *A simpler version for 3- and 4-year olds:*
> - *Fingerpaint arcs.*
> - *Allow paint to dry.*
> - *Take painting out in the rain for a minute.*
> - *Note pattern the raindrops make.*

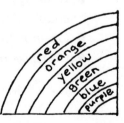

Related Activities

1. NURSERY RHYME:

Can be sung to the tune of "Frère Jacques."

I HEAR THUNDER, I HEAR THUNDER,

(stamp feet on floor)

*MARK, DON'T YOU, *MARK, DON'T YOU?
PITTER-PATTER RAINDROPS (indicate rain with fingers)
PITTER-PATTER RAINDROPS
I'M WET THROUGH. (shake from head to toes)
SO ARE YOU! (point to neighbor)

*Repeat substituting children's names in your group.

2. VERSE:

PITTER-PAT, PITTER-PAT, OH SO MANY HOURS,
ALTHOUGH IT KEEPS ME IN THE HOUSE,
IT'S VERY GOOD FOR FLOWERS.

3. SONG:

RAIN, RAIN, (wiggle fingers)
GO AWAY. (motion away with hand)
COME AGAIN (motion toward you with hand)
ANOTHER DAY. (clap hands 4 times)

Sing the song through, using the actions. Repeat the song, only remain silent through the first line while doing the actions. Continue in this manner until you remain silent for the whole song, doing the actions only.

4. OUTDOOR FUN:

On a sunny day you can make your own rainbow.

- *Have a friend hold a hose up, making a fine spray of water in front of you.*
- *Stand with your back to the sun.*
- *Look at the spray of water, and you should see a rainbow.*

A SLICE OF LIFE!

MATERIALS:
- Red, white, and green construction paper
- Watermelon seeds
- White glue
- Q-Tips (optional)
- Scissors

PREPARATION:
- Cut out three semi-circles: one green, a slightly smaller white one, and a slightly smaller red one (see the diagram). Provide one set of shapes per child.
- Rinse off watermelon seeds and spread them out to dry.

CHILD'S PLAY:
- Glue the white semi-circle onto the green semi-circle.
- Glue the red semi-circle onto the white one.
- Squeeze drops of white glue onto the red semi-circle. (Or use a Q-Tip to dab on spots of glue.)
- Press watermelon seeds onto the glue.

Related Activities

1. NATURE STUDY:

Give each child a slice of watermelon to eat. What remains when you're finished eating?

a) Seeds—Let the seeds dry out and plant them indoors (three to a large paper cup). You can later transplant the seedlings to the garden.

b) Rind—Put the rind in a compost heap, and it can be used later to help nurture the seedlings you transplant to the garden. NOTHING LEFT FOR THE GARBAGE CAN!

2. VERSE:

RED, WHITE, GREEN,
WHAT DOES IT MEAN?
THE BIGGEST SLICE OF WATERMELON
YOU'VE EVER SEEN!

Children hide their crafts behind their backs for the first two lines, then proudly show them on line 3.

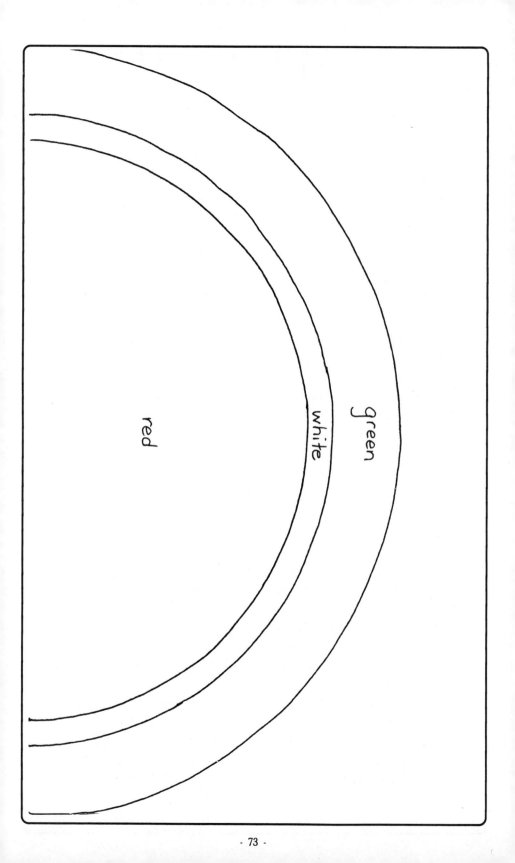

red

white

green

DRIPPING ICICLES

MATERIALS:

- Icicles (natural or homemade)
- Fingerpaint paper
  (or white glossy paper)
- Powdered tempera, red
- Empty salt shaker
- Waxed paper
- Glue
- Black marker
- Scissors

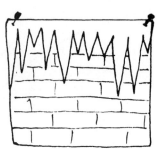

PREPARATION:

- *Draw a brick wall on the fingerpaint paper.*
- *Trace and cut a row of icicles from waxed paper. (Older children will want to do these first two steps themselves.)*
- *Place tempera in salt shaker.*
- *If natural icicles are not available, make your own in Popsicle molds or use an ice cube tray and Popsicle sticks.*

CHILD'S PLAY:

- *Go on an outdoor excursion and find an icicle.*
- *Rub your icicle over the surface of the wall drawing, to moisten the paper (you may want to keep your mittens on).*
- *Sprinkle tempera on the wall.*
- *Rub your icicle over the dry paint on the entire wall and watch it transform into a brilliant red.*
- *Let the paint and paper dry. (Use the time to try related activities.)*
- *Use black marker to outline the wall and bricks.*
- *Glue the row of icicles along the top edge of wall.*
- *Draw in finishing touches such as a sun. (My older son, Mark, added his own creative flair by drawing sad faces on all the icicles and a happy face on the sun.)*

Related Activities

Row of Icicles

1. POEM: *"The Icicle"*

THE ICICLE HUNG ON THE RED BRICK WALL,
AND HE SAID TO THE SUN, "I DON'T LIKE YOU AT ALL,"
DRIP, DRIP, DRIP.
BUT THE SUN SAID "DEAR, YOU'VE A SAUCY TONGUE.
I MUST REMIND YOU, I'M OLD AND YOU'RE YOUNG."
DRIP, DRIP, DRIP.
BUT THE ICICLE ONLY CRIED THE MORE
WHILE THE BRIGHT SUN SHONE ON HIM
   JUST AS BEFORE,
DRIP, DRIP, DRIP.
UNTIL AT THE END OF THE WINTER DAY
HE HAD CRIED HIS POOR LITTLE SELF AWAY,
DRIP, DRIP, DRIP!

Children can provide the "drip, drip, drip" while you tell them this poem.

2. SNACK TIME: *An Icy Treat*

- *Drop fruit pieces (strawberry, banana slices, etc.) into each section of the ice cube tray.*
- *Fill the tray with water or juice. Freeze the contents.*
- *Add the cubes to cold drinks for a tasty treat.*

3. EXPERIMENT:

- *Fill a glass jar with ice cubes and cover the jar with the lid.*
- *Leave the jar to sit at room temperature for about 15 minutes.*
- *What has happened to the ice cubes?*
- *What has happened to the outside of the jar?*

SNOWSCAPE

MATERIALS:
- Blue, green, and brown construction paper
- Scissors
- White glue
- Small paintbrushes (or Q-Tips)
- Salt and salt shakers

PREPARATION:
- *Cut triangles from the green construction paper. Provide at least 7 triangles per child. Use different shades of green paper if available.*

CHILD'S PLAY:
- *To make the ground for your snowscape, cut a strip approx. 3" x 11" (8 cm x 30 cm) from the brown paper. (This is a great first cutting experience since you can create flat or hilly terrain.)*
- *Glue brown paper onto the bottom of blue paper.*
- *Glue green triangles (trees), with the points up, onto the paper. Try overlapping the triangles.*
- *Use a small brush or Q-Tip to brush glue here and there on trees and ground.*
- *Shake salt on the glue.*
- *Shake off the excess salt.*
- *Using a glue bottle, squeeze drops of glue onto blue sky. (This will harden into little snowflakes.)*

VARIATION: Use dried coconut instead of salt to create a blizzard.

HINT: Do this craft on a tray and cleanup is easy.

Related Activities

1. SONG:

Sing this song to the tune of "London Bridge Is Falling Down."

*SNOWFLAKES WHIRLING ALL AROUND,
ALL AROUND, ALL AROUND;
SNOWFLAKES WHIRLING ALL AROUND,
UNTIL THEY COVER ALL THE GROUND.*

Children whirl around and then fall to the ground.

2. SNOW PAINTING:

*Mix food coloring with water and pour the mixture into
squeeze bottles. Use as many different colors as you
have. Each child can take a bottle outside to create
colorful designs in the snow. Watch for the melting
process in the days ahead and see what happens to the
rainbow of colors.*

3. OLD SAYING:

*IF FEBRUARY BRINGS DRIFTS OF SNOW,
THERE WILL BE GOOD SUMMER CROPS TO HOE.*

4. OUTDOOR FUN:

*All you need is a snowy day, black construction paper,
and a magnifying glass. Cut the paper into squares of
approx. 4″ × 4″ (10 cm × 10 cm). Refrigerate the squares
for a few hours. Take the squares outside and hold them
level to catch a few snowflakes. Examine the snowflakes
under a magnifying glass. Wow! Each one is a different
pattern!*

—DAFFODIL, DAFFODIL—

MATERIALS:
- Blue, brown, yellow, and green construction paper
- Yellow egg carton
- White glue
- Pinking shears (optional)

PREPARATION:
- Cut petal shapes from the yellow paper (see the diagram).
- Cut leaves and stems from the green paper. Provide four or five leaves per child.
- Cut bulb from the brown paper (see the diagram).
- Cut a single "eggcup" section from the egg carton. You can use pinking shears to trim around the edges. Allow one section per child.

CHILD'S PLAY:
- Glue bulb at the bottom of the blue paper, in the center.
- Glue on stem; the lower end should touch the bulb.
- Glue on leaves; attach bases of leaves to the bulb.
- Glue petal shapes to the top of the stem. (If you glue only the center, you can curl petals up later to give a realistic effect.)
- Glue eggcup to the middle of petals.
- Cut a strip of brown paper approx. 9" × 3" (23 cm × 7 cm). This strip will be the ground, so it's fine if it's uneven.
- Glue brown strip, along top edge only, and stick it onto the blue paper about an inch (4 cm) above where the leaves join the bulb.
- Now you can take a peek at what is happening under the ground by folding back the brown paper.

Related Activities

1. VERSE: *"Daffodil, Daffodil"*

IN THE SNOWING AND THE BLOWING
AND THE CRUEL SLEET,
TINY FLOWERS ARE GROWING
DEEP BENEATH OUR FEET.
DAFFODIL, DAFFODIL, SAY CAN YOU HEAR?
WINTER IS OVER AND SPRINGTIME IS HERE.

2. FINGERPLAY:

PITTER PATTER RAINDROPS   (wiggle fingers)
DANCE AND RUN AND PLAY,
      (wiggle fingers, moving them in all directions)

FALL UPON THE DAFFODILS   (wiggle fingers downward)
ON A NICE SPRING DAY.

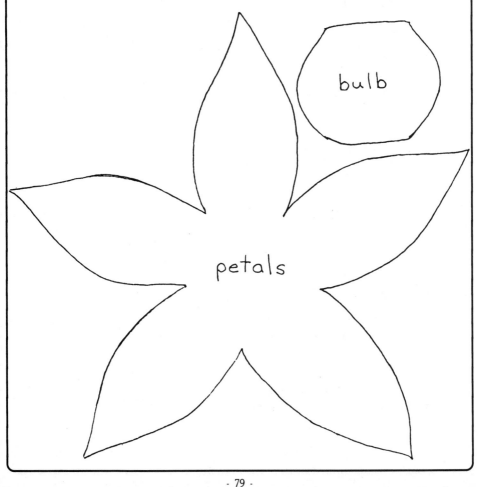

- 79 -

MY BEAN GARDEN

MATERIALS:
- Egg cartons
- Potting soil
- Bucket
- Spoons
- Bean seeds
- Cardboard
- Tape
- Small watering can
- Sharp pencils
- Scissors

PREPARATION:
- *Provide one egg carton per child. Cut lids off egg cartons. Set the lids aside to be used later as trays.*
- *Cut strips of cardboard to approx. 1" × 8" (3 cm × 20 cm) to serve as labels. For example, a label might say "JONATHAN'S BEAN GARDEN."*
- *Place soil in the bucket.*

CHILD'S PLAY:
- *Use a sharp pencil to poke a hole for drainage in the bottom of each "eggcup."*
- *Set the carton lid under the egg carton to form a tray.*
- *Spoon soil into each eggcup.*
- *Poke your finger into each eggcup to create a hole.*
- *Drop a bean seed into each hole.*
- *Cover the seed with soil.*
- *Sprinkle the soil with water.*
- *Use the pencil to write a label on the cardboard. Tape the cardboard label to the flap at the edge of the egg carton.*
- *Place your bean garden in a sunny spot and sprinkle with water daily. (Add just enough to moisten the soil.)*
- *After beans have grown to about 3" (7 cm) in height, transplant them to an outdoor garden.*

Related Activities

1. SONG:

Sing to the tune of "Here We Go 'Round the Mulberry Bush."

WE ARE GOING TO PLANT A BEAN,
PLANT A BEAN, PLANT A BEAN.
WE ARE GOING TO PLANT A BEAN,
IN OUR LITTLE GREEN GARDEN.

FIRST WE MAKE A HOLE WITH OUR FINGER...

THEN WE DROP THE BEAN SEED IN...

NEXT WE SPRINKLE THE WATER ON...

Continue with suggestions from the children for other verses.

2. GAME: *Beanbag Beat*

Children sit in a circle. Use a musical instrument such as a drum to establish a beat. The children pass the beanbag to the beat. (Once the children have caught on, vary the beat from slow to fast.) When the instrument stops, whoever is holding the beanbag is given a turn to establish a beat. Continue until everyone has had a turn playing the instrument.

3. SONG:

OATS AND BEANS AND BARLEY GROW
OATS AND BEANS AND BARLEY GROW.
NOT YOU, NOR I, NOR ANYONE KNOWS
HOW OATS AND BEANS AND BARLEY GROW.

FIRST THE FARMER PLANTS THE SEED,
STANDS UP TALL AND TAKES HIS EASE,
STAMPS HIS FEET AND CLAPS HIS HANDS
AND TURNS AROUND TO SEE HIS LAND.

4. STORY TIME: *"Jack and the Beanstalk"*

There is nothing in which the birds differ more from man
than the way in which they can build
and yet leave a landscape as it was before.

Robert Lynd

CARING FOR NATURE

ENVIRO-BUG PUPPET

MATERIALS:

- Socks
- Cardboard
- Craft glue
- Felt scraps
- Pipe cleaners, each approx. 12″ (30 cm) long
- Scissors

PREPARATION:

- *Cut oval shape out of cardboard and fold it in half (see Diagram A). Cut as many ovals as socks.*
- *Spread glue on the outside of one oval and press the oval into the toe of a sock, fold first. (I indented the toe of the sock first, then pressed the cardboard inside.) Prepare all socks.*
- *Use scissors to poke two holes into each sock (see Diagram B).*
- *Cut pipe cleaners in half.*
- *Cut out features for bugs from felt scraps.*

CHILD'S PLAY:

- *Glue tongue to cardboard mouth.*
- *Glue on felt features to create your own unique enviro-bug.*
- *Thread pipe cleaner through holes in sock, for antennae.*
- *Wear your enviro-bug on your hand. Open and close its mouth. Look around your neighborhood for litter— your enviro-bug can grasp it in its mouth. (We found plenty of "food" at the local park.)*

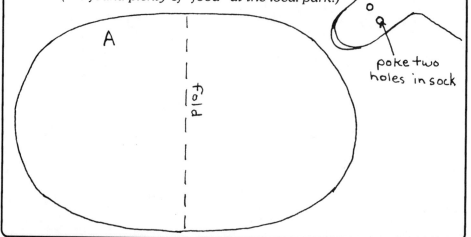

A

fold

B

poke two holes in sock

Related Activities

1. SONG:

Sing to the tune of "I'm a Little Teapot." Wear your enviro-bug puppet, and it can sing along with you.

I'M A HUNGRY ENVIRO-BUG, AS YOU CAN SEE,
I LIKE TO EAT UP LITTER, WITH A ONE, TWO, THREE.
THAT WILL KEEP OUR WORLD AS CLEAN
   AS IT CAN BE,
FOR PLANTS AND ANIMALS AND YOU AND ME.

2. PLAYDOUGH FUN:

See recipe on p. 53. Use several different colors of playdough and pipe cleaners to create imaginative, colorful bugs. The children can create bodies with one color of playdough and add features by using contrasting colors. Pieces of pipe cleaners make interesting legs, antennae, and wings.

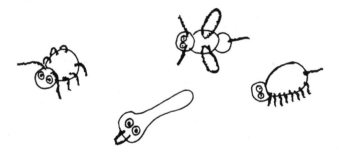

3. VERSE:

Children can wear their enviro-bug puppets and respond in unison, on alternate lines, with "You're a Litterbug!"

IF YOU THROW LITTER IN THE GRASS,
YOU'RE A LITTERBUG!
IF ON THE STREET YOU LEAVE SOME GLASS,
YOU'RE A LITTERBUG!
IF YOU THROW LITTER IN THE AIR,
YOU'RE A LITTERBUG!
IF YOU THROW LITTER ANYWHERE,
YOU'RE A LITTERBUG!

FIRE'S BURNING

MATERIALS:

- Black construction paper
- Orange tissue paper (or crepe paper)
- Glue
- Twigs
- White chalk (optional)
- Scissors
- Razor knife (optional)

PREPARATION:

- *Trace flames onto black construction paper and then cut them out. You may want to use a razor knife.*
- *Cut orange tissue paper to make a square of approx. 6" (15 cm). Provide one square per child.*

CHILD'S PLAY:

- *Glue tissue paper onto black paper so that it covers the holes (flames).*
- *Turn black paper over, and glue twigs underneath the flames.*
- *Use white chalk to draw stick people standing around the campfire.*
- *Display in a window, and the light will make the fire shine brightly.*

Related Activities

1. ACTION VERSE:

FIRE! FIRE! YOU MUST BEWARE,
FIRE! FIRE! ALWAYS TAKE CARE,
TO SOAK IT WITH WATER AND COVER WITH DIRT,
SO PEOPLE, ANIMALS, AND FORESTS DON'T GET HURT.
FIRE! FIRE! YOU MUST BEWARE
FIRE! FIRE! ALWAYS TAKE CARE.

This verse can be sung to "Baa, Baa, Black Sheep."
Suggested Actions:
Lines 1 and 2—Raise arms in alarm, waggle "pointer" finger.
Lines 3 and 4—Wiggle fingers downward.
Lines 5 and 6—Repeat actions for lines 1 and 2.

2. CAMPFIRE SONG:

FIRE'S BURNING, FIRE'S BURNING,
DRAW NEARER, DRAW NEARER,
IN THE GLOAMING, IN THE GLOAMING,
COME SING AND BE MERRY.

"RECYCLE ME" CRAFT BOX

MATERIALS:

- Medium cardboard boxes
- Glue
- Brushes for glue
- Recycled paper: gift wrap, tissue paper, newspaper, magazines, wallpaper, wax paper, cardboard, etc.
- Scissors (or razor knife)
- Small container or containers for glue

PREPARATION:

- *Provide one box per child. Cut off lid flaps from the boxes.*
- *Cut or tear recycled paper into small squares of approx. 4" (10 cm).*
- *Pour glue into small container or containers.*

CHILD'S PLAY:

- *Brush glue onto one side of the box and stick on various types of recycled paper. Overlap papers and place them at different angles.*
- *Repeat until all four sides of the box are covered in a collage of recycled paper.*

  OPTIONAL:
  Use a strip of recycled cardboard to print the label "RECYCLE ME," and glue the label onto the box as a reminder.

- *Now fill your "Recycle Me" Craft Box with all those great household items that can be used in craft projects. (See related activity #1.)*

Related Activities

1. TREASURE HUNT:

("One man's junk is another man's treasure.")
Take your craft box and search around home and
neighborhood for items to recycle.

Suggestions:

- *Kitchen: egg cartons, empty paper towel rolls, milk cartons, tin cans, etc.*
- *Living room: old magazines, catalogues, newspapers, etc.*
- *Sewing room: discarded ribbon, buttons, beads, yarn, string, felt scraps, clothespins, etc.*
- *Neighborhood: Popsicle sticks, plastic bottle, bottle caps, boxes of all sizes, etc.*

2. SIMPLE RECYCLING IDEAS:

a) Children's gift wrap: Save the weekend comics that come
with the newspaper. They make excellent gift wrap for
children's birthday presents.

b) Drum: We made a simple drum for our 4-year-old from
a large tin can, inner tube of a tire, and twine.
It was made completely from items
destined for the garbage and had
a much better sound than the
commercial ones (which drive
parents crazy with their loud,
tinny noise).

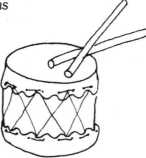

c) Button spinner: Thread a 3-ft. (1-meter) piece of string
through the two holes of a fairly large button. Tie the ends of
string together to create a loop with the button in the middle.
Place your index fingers in the string at either end of the loop,
and twirl the button around in a circle several times. When
string is wound tight, pull outward with your hands, and the
button will spin and hum.

RECYCLED HEARTS

MATERIALS:
- Cardboard
- Waxed paper (recycled material)
- Red tissue paper
- Glue
- Cooking oil
- One-hole punch
- Brushes for oil
- String
- Scissors

PREPARATION:
- *Cut cardboard into a heart frame. (See the diagram on the opposite page.)*
- *Cut out a waxed paper heart the same size as the cardboard frame.*
- *Glue waxed paper heart to the frame.*

CHILD'S PLAY:
- *Tear tissue paper into small pieces approx. 1/2" (2 cm) square.*
- *Brush a generous amount of cooking oil over waxed paper heart.*
- *Place tissue paper pieces on the oil until waxed paper heart is completely covered.*
- *Punch a hole at the top of the heart.*
- *Tie a string to the heart for easy suspension from a Celebration Tree (p. 50) or any other appropriate site.*

Related Activities

1. ANIMAL SHAPES:
Cut several different sizes of hearts out of construction paper, and the children can have fun creating different animal shapes.

2. CIRCLE-TIME GAME:

Make large red and pink hearts from construction paper and print an action on the back—e.g., hop, touch your toes, crawl. Set the hearts in a circle, plain side up, on the floor. Make sure there is one for each child to sit on. The children can take turns revealing their action, and then the whole group can do the activity described.

3. MUSICAL HUGS:

Play some lively music while the children dance and skip around the room. When the music stops, the children find someone to hug. (If there's an odd number of children, three people can hug—or four or five, for that matter.)

4. STORY TIME: *"I'll Love You Forever"*

by Robert Munsch

— FOOD-CHAIN MOBILE —

MATERIALS:
- Construction paper (black, yellow, and white)
- Yellow crayon
- Old magazines
- Glue
- String
- Scissors

PREPARATION:
- *Cut out circles in graduating sizes from black paper.*
- *With the scissors, poke a hole at the top and bottom of each circle, except the largest circle, which needs a hole at the top only.*
- *Cut chicken shapes, two per child, from yellow paper.*

CHILD'S PLAY:
- *Cut out faces of two people from a magazine and glue one on each side of the large circle.*
- *Cut egg shapes from white paper and glue several on each side of the next largest circle.*
- *On the third circle, glue a chicken shape on either side.*
- *With yellow crayon, make dots all over both sides of smallest circle. The dots represent grain.*
- *Tie string to largest circle and then thread it in and out of the other circles in order of size. Space circles about 4" (10 cm) apart along the string. Help from an adult can make the job easier.*
- *After an adult suspends the mobile from the ceiling, you can admire your work.*

Related Activities

1. PAPER CHAIN:

Prepare strips of different-colored construction paper. Print on each strip the name of a plant or animal in a food chain: for example, leaf, caterpillar, frog, snake, large bird.

Children glue strips, in order of food chain, to create a paper chain. This will help show that what happens at one end of the chain will affect the entire chain.

2. CAMPFIRE SONG:

Sing to the tune of "There's a Little White Duck."

> *THERE'S A LITTLE BLACK BUG*
>   *FLOATING ON THE WATER.*
> *A LITTLE BLACK BUG DOING WHAT HE OUGHTER.*
> *HE TOOK A BITE OF A LILY PAD,*
> *WIGGLED HIS FEELERS, AND SAID, "I'M GLAD*
> *I'M A LITTLE BLACK BUG FLOATING ON THE WATER.*
> *CHIRP, CHIRP, CHIRP."*

> *THERE'S A LITTLE GREEN FROG*
>   *SWIMMING IN THE WATER.*
> *A LITTLE GREEN FROG DOING WHAT HE OUGHTER.*
> *HE JUMPED RIGHT OFF THE LILY PAD.*
> *HE ATE THE LITTLE BUG AND HE SAID, "I'M GLAD*
> *I'M A LITTLE GREEN FROG SWIMMING IN THE WATER*
> *CROAK, CROAK, CROAK."*

> *THERE'S A LITTLE RED SNAKE*
>   *LYING ON THE WATER.*
> *A LITTLE RED SNAKE DOING WHAT HE OUGHTER.*
> *HIS HUNGER WAS GETTING MIGHTY BAD,*
> *WHEN HE GULPED THE FROG AND HE SAID,*
>   *"I'M GLAD*
> *I'M A LITTLE RED SNAKE LYING ON THE WATER.*
> *SSSS! SSSS! SSSS!"*

3. CREATIVE MOVEMENT: *Animal Imitations*

> *CAN YOU CRAWL LIKE A SNAKE?*
> *CAN YOU STRUT LIKE A HEN?*
> *CAN YOU FLY LIKE A BIRD?*
> *CAN YOU HOP LIKE A FROG?*
> *ETC.*

SEASONAL INDEX

FILL IN AND MAIL... TODAY

PRIMA PUBLISHING
P.O. Box 1260JWB2
Rocklin, CA 95677

Use Your VISA/MC And Order By Phone
(916) 786-0449
Mon.-Fri. 9-4 PST (12-7 EST)

Dear Prima,
I'd like to order copies of the following titles:

_____ copies of *Making the Grade* (available
September 1992) at $10.95 each for a total of . . . . _____

_____ copies *Raising Self-Reliant Children in a
Self-Indulgent World* at $9.95 each for a total of . . . . _____

_____ copies *Look What I Made!* at $9.95 each for a total of . . . _____

_____ copies *Look What I Made Now!* at $9.95 each
for a total of . . . . _____

Subtotal _____

Shipping ($3 for first item,
$1.50 for each additional item) _____

7¼% Sales Tax (CA only) _____

Total Order _____

_____ Check enclosed for $_____, payable to Prima Publishing
Charge my _____ MasterCard _____ VISA

Account No. _____ Exp. Date _____

Signature _____

Your Name _____

Address _____

City/State/Zip _____

Daytime Telephone _____

GUARANTEE
YOU MUST BE SATISFIED
You get a 30-day, 100% money-back guarantee on all books

Thank you for your order